to: moms

from: Matt

I LOVE YOU
mom

**Published by Sellers Publishing, Inc.**

161 John Roberts Road, South Portland, ME 04106

Visit us at www.sellerspublishing.com • E-mail: rsp@rsvp.com

© 2016 Sellers Publishing, Inc.

Art and design © 2016 Amylee Weeks

Courtesy of MHS Licensing

Compiled by Robin Haywood

ISBN-13: 978-1-4162-4579-7

Printed and bound in China.

10  9  8  7  6  5  4  3  2  1

# I LOVE YOU mom

art & design by amylee weeks

SELLERS
PUBLISHING

[ MOTHERHOOD is ]
the biggest gamble
in the world.
It is the glorious
life force.
It is huge and scary
it is an act of
infinite
optimism.

- Gilda Radner

Because you
always believed in me,
I learned to believe
in myself.

A MOM'S HUG LASTS LONG AFTER SHE LETS GO.

- Anonymous

A MOM FORGIVES
ALL OUR FAULTS,
NOT TO MENTION
ONE OR TWO
WE DON'T EVEN HAVE.

*- Robert Brault*

For all the times
I needed, and received
your forgiveness,
thank you.

THE HEART OF A
*mother*
IS A DEEP OCEAN
AT THE BOTTOM
OF WHICH YOU WILL
ALWAYS FIND
*forgiveness.*

- Honoré de Balzac

To describe my

# MOTHER

would be to write

about a

hurricane

in its

PERFECT POWER

Or the climbing,

falling colors of a

# RAINBOW.

– Maya Angelou

WHEN IT COMES TO

LOVE

MOM'S THE WORD.

- *Anonymous*

Who in their
infinite wisdom
decreed that
Little League
uniforms
be white?
Certainly not
a Mother.

— ERMA BOMBECK

Motherhood can be messy.
You were never afraid
to get your hands dirty.

Thank you for always making me feel safe.

GOD COULD NOT BE
everywhere
SO HE CREATED
mothers.

- JEWISH PROVERB

If I have done
anything in life
worth
attention,
I feel sure
that I inherited
the disposition
from my
MOTHER.

- Booker T. Washington

So many of
the good things
in my life can
be attributed
to you.

We are as one.

# MOTHER
the ribbons
of your love
are woven
around my
heart.

- Anonymous

*You inspired me,*

*MOM,*

*to pursue*

*my*

DREAMS.

*— Anonymous*

Yes, Mother.
I can see
you are flawed.
You have not
hidden it.
That is your
greatest gift
to me.

- Alice Walker

Thank you.

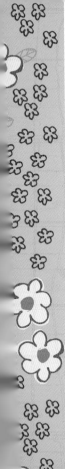

MY MOM IS A
NEVER-ENDING
SONG IN MY HEART
OF COMFORT, HAPPINESS, AND BEING.
I MAY SOMETIMES
FORGET THE WORDS,
BUT I ALWAYS REMEMBER
THE TUNE.

-Terri Guillemets

# A MOTHER IS THE TRUEST FRIEND WE HAVE...

– Washington Irving

My mother
was a
personal friend
of God's.
They had ongoing
conversations.

- Della Reese

There is
only one
pretty child
in the world,
and
every mother
has it.

- Chinese Proverb

You nurtured
my heart
and nourished
my soul.

I don't know
what it is about
FOOD
your mother
makes for you...
pancakes, meat loaf,
tuna salad...
but it carries
a taste of
MEMORY

- Mitch Albom

EVERYBODY
*wants to*
*save the earth;*
*nobody wants*
*to help*
MOM
*do the dishes.*

- P. J. O'Rourke

I AM
SO
BLESSED

There is no
influence
so powerful
as that of the

# MOTHER

- Sarah Josepha Hale

A MOTHER
UNDERSTANDS
WHAT A
CHILD
DOES NOT SAY.

- JEWISH PROVERB

You and I have a connection that goes far beyond words.

*No matter how old a mother is, she watches her middle-aged children for signs of improvement.*

— Florida Scott-Maxwell

YOU INSPIRE ME
TO ALWAYS LOOK
FOR WAYS
I CAN GROW.

You are the star
by which I navigate
through life.

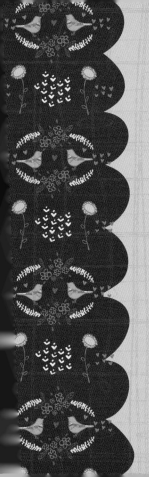

MOTHERS
and their
CHILDREN
are in a
category all their own.
There's no
BOND
so strong
in the
entire world.

- Gail Tsukiyama

My goal in life
is to make you proud

Mom,
the best
thing
about me
is
you.

- Anonymous

mother

first friend, best friend,
forever friend

What is a
MOM
but the
SUNSHINE
of our days
and the
NORTH STAR
of our nights.

- Robert Brault

It is not
until you
become a

MOTHER

that your
judgment
slowly turns to
compassion
and
understanding.

- Erma Bombeck

You are in my thoughts and in my heart, each and every day.

I am sure
that if the
🦋 MOTHERS 🦋
of various nations
could meet,
there would be
no more wars.

- E. M. Forster

Thank you, mom, for
slaying the monsters
that lived under my bed.

- Anonymous

No one
in the world
can take
the place
of your mother.
Right or wrong,
from her viewpoint
you are
always right.

- Harry Truman

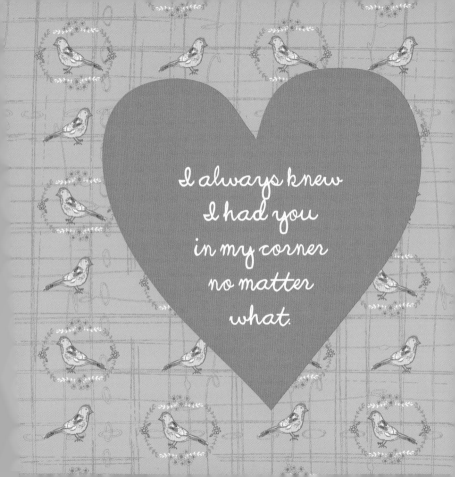

I always knew
I had you
in my corner
no matter
what.

Most mothers
are
instinctive
philosophers.

- Harriet Beecher Stowe

A mother's
love
is
bliss.

– Erich Fromm

THINKING
OF YOU
LIFTS
MY SPIRIT.